Professional Generalship
and the USAWC Curriculum

John B. B. Trussell

Included are the following Collections:

Budget of The United States Government
Presidential Documents
United States Code
Education Reports from ERIC
GAO Reports
History of Bills
House Rules and Manual
Public and Private Laws

Code of Federal Regulations
Congressional Documents
Economic Indicators
Federal Register
Government Manuals
House Journal
Privacy act Issuances
Statutes at Large

US ARMY WAR COLLEGE
Carlisle Barracks, Pennsylvania 17013

AWCIR   15 October 1971

MEMORANDUM THRU: DI
                  DCOMDT

FOR: COMDT

SUBJECT: "Professional Generalship" and the USAWC Curriculum

1. Reference: Memorandum, Chairman, DR&S, "Definition of 'Professional Generalship'," 25 June 1971 (Appendix A to Inclosure 1).

2. At Inclosure 1 is my study on "professional generalship" and its support by the USAWC curriculum.

3. The study delineated "professional generalship" in terms of what US Army generals do, examining

    a. The different assignments currently filled by general officers;

    b. The types of assignments held by O-9's and O-10's throughout their service as general officers;

    c. The types of activities common to general officers, regardless of specific assignment.

4. The study determined that:

    a. Performance in approximately half of the assignments currently filled by general officers depends primarily for its formal professional educational preparation on Senior Service College curricula.

    b. At least half of the total general officer service of the typical O-9 and O-10 has been spent in assignments for which the Senior Service Colleges are the primary source of formal professional educational preparation.

    c. The USAWC curriculum addresses in considerable detail and with apparent adequacy the broad subjects related to the performance of the general officer assignments referred to above (i.e., the assignments which are not primarily supported by the branch schools and the Command and General Staff College).

    d. Of nine broad types of activities identified by the study as common to general officers, regardless of specific assignment, the USAWC curriculum addresses five with apparent adequacy, but the remaining four are covered either inadequately or not at all.

5. In order to correct these deficiencies, the study recommends incorporation into the curriculum of:

    a. A panel from the Office of the Chief of Legislative Liaison on the subject of relations with the Congress;

    b. A panel from the Office of the Chief of Information on the subject of relations with the information media;

    c. A subcourse on legal relationships and responsibilities of senior commanders;

    d. Increased emphasis on substantive and technical quality of oral communication, entailing modification of the system of student evaluation.

1 Incl
as

                        JOHN B. B. TRUSSELL, JR.
                        Colonel, ADA
                        Chairman, Department of
                        Research and Studies

INTRODUCTION

1. The basis for this study is provided by the memorandum at Appendix A.

    a. To meet the provisions of that memorandum, this study is organized in four parts:

        (1) Part I addresses the question, "To what types of duties are US Army generals assigned?" It then considers the ways in which the US Army War College curriculum addresses the requirements for formal education for "professional generalship" as delineated by the types of assignments which US Army generals fill.

        (2) Part II addresses the question, "What specific types of activity are common to the duties of general officers, regardless of assignment?" It then considers the ways in which the US Army War College curriculum addresses the requirements for "professional generalship" as delineated by these types of activity.

        (3) Part III provides general conclusions relevant to both of the preceding assessments of "professional generalship."

        (4) Part IV offers recommendations.

    b. The memorandum at Appendix A proposed a further question: "What system of values should we adopt in distinguishing good or bad leaders from others, and what behavioral patterns characterize those who are 'good leaders'?" Subsequent reflection has led to the conclusion that this question, involving as it does issues of character, personality, and style, was not completely relevant to this study, and therefore was omitted.

2. The term "Professional generalship" has many possible applications. This study uses the term to refer to what US Army general officers do; it does not address the question of how (i.e., with what styles or by what techniques) they perform their assignments.

3. Clearly, in the performance of any of his assignments a general officer will draw on the totality of his professional educational background. However, some assignments will demand greater reliance upon the background provided by one part of the Army's professional educational program than upon other parts. This study addresses "professional generalship" in terms of the background for its practice which is or should be provided by the US Army War College.

1

4. No attempt is made to consider the propriety or desirability of orienting the USAWC curriculum on preparing officers for "professional generalship." Current experience indicates that only some 20 percent of USAWC graduates become generals. It is not possible to predict which specific USAWC students will become generals; however, virtually all USAWC graduates will eventually occupy positions in which, either as generals or advisers to generals, they will be concerned with the practice of "professional generalship."

PART I

TYPES OF DUTIES TO WHICH US ARMY GENERALS ARE ASSIGNED

1. This portion of the study is based on data pertaining to all US Army general officers and promotable colonels on active duty as of 1 May 1971, with the following exceptions:

    a. General officers carried in the Holding Detachment, OCofSA;

    b. General officers of the Reserve Components assigned to the National Guard Bureau and the Office of the Chief, Army Reserve;

    c. The Special Adviser to the President on Manpower Mobilization (General Lewis B. Hershey); and

    d. The Secretary of the American Battle Monuments Commission.

2. Assignments were examined in terms of the types of assignments currently filled by general officers; and the types of assignments held by selected general officers throughout their service as general officers.

    a. Types of assignments currently filled by general officers.

        (1) The source of data on current assignments of US Army general officers was the 1 May 1971 General Officers' Assignment List. The objective of this examination was to identify and categorize the positions to which general officers of each particular grade are assigned. Hence, any reasonably current issue of the General Officers' Assignment List was considered valid for the purpose at hand.

        (2) The assignments filled by US Army general officers as of 1 May 1971 were categorized according to the dominant type of function involved in each assignment—i.e., the function distinguishing each category from the others. The five functional categories thus derived are shown in Figure 1, below:

CATEGORY TITLE	DOMINANT FUNCTIONS
CATEGORY I: POLICY/STRATEGY	ASSIGNMENTS DEALING PRIMARILY WITH MATTERS OF INTERNATIONAL, NATIONAL, DOD, JOINT, AND DA POLICY AND/OR STRATEGY.
CATEGORY II: MANAGEMENT/ADMIN-ISTRATION	ASSIGNMENTS CONCERNED WITH THE PRO-CUREMENT AND ALLOCATION OF RESOURCES, AND DIRECTION OF THE UTILIZATION OF THOSE RESOURCES OTHER THAN IN A PRIMARILY TACTICAL SENSE.
CATEGORY III: MAAGs, MISSIONS, MILITARY DIPLOMACY	ASSIGNMENTS, OTHER THAN THOSE INVOLV-ING FORMULATION OF OVERALL POLICY OR STRATEGY, IN WHICH INTERNATIONAL MILITARY COOPERATION IS THE DOMINANT CONSIDERATION.
CATEGORY IV: OPERATIONS/TACTICS	ASSIGNMENTS IN WHICH THE PREDOMINANT ACTIVITY INVOLVES TACTICAL MILITARY OPERATIONS IN THE FIELD OR TRAINING THEREFOR (LESS BRANCH MATERIAL ASSIGNMENTS).
CATEGORY V: BRANCH MATERIAL	ASSIGNMENTS RESERVED TO GENERAL OFFICERS OF A SPECIFIC ARM OR SERVICE

Figure 1. Functional Categories of General Officer Assignments.

(3) For editorial convenience, the categories themselves were grouped according to the principal source of professional educational background upon which their incumbents are called to draw in the performance of their duties. As illustrated in Figure 2, page 4, the assignments falling in Categories I, II, and III (Policy/Strategy; Management/Administration; and MAAGs, Missions, Military Diplomacy) can be said, generally speaking, to draw extensively for formal professional education on the

3

Senior Service College curricula. Similarly, assignments falling in
Categories IV and V (Operations/Tactics; and Branch Material) draw primarily on the branch schools and the Command and General Staff College.
A detailed listing of assignments by category is included in the discussion
in Appendix B.

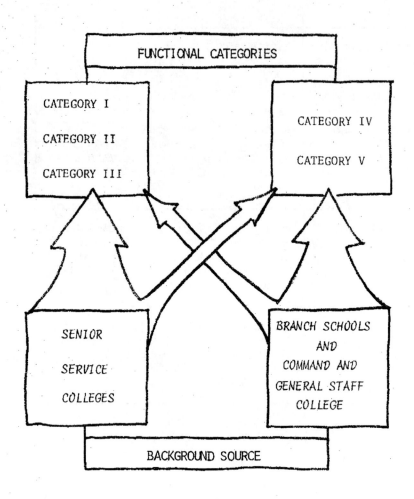

Figure 2. Sources of professional educational background for functional
categories of general officer assignments.

(4) The general officers on active duty as of 1 May 1971 were serving in the various categories as shown in Table I, "Distribution of General Officers by Grade," at Appendix C, "Tables." This table shows that general officers' assignments are almost equally divided between the categories depending primarily on the Senior Service College curricula and those depending chiefly on other aspects of the Army educational system—Categories I, II, and III account for 50.3 percent of the general officer assignments, while Categories IV and V account for 49.7 percent. However, the distribution by grade is somewhat different: while slightly more than half (52.4 percent) of 0-7's and 0-8's are serving in Category IV and Category V assignments, barely more than one-fourth (27.6 percent) of the 0-9's and 0-10's are serving in assignments falling into those categories.

b. Types of assignments held by general officers throughout their service as general officers.

(1) To establish the pattern of general officer assignments, the official resumes of the service careers of 58 selected individuals were examined to determine the number of months of general officer service spent in each of the five established categories. These totals were then averaged to determine the assignment pattern of a composite US Army general.

(2) This portion of the study restricted its consideration to all 0-9's and 0-10's (less General Hershey) on active duty as of 1 May 1971. The restriction to general officers of these two grades was adopted for the following reasons:

(a) To reveal a meaningful pattern, an individual's length of service as a general officer must be sufficiently great to permit him to have a substantial number of assignments. 0-7's who do not become 0-8's will typically hold only three, or even fewer, assignments prior to reaching mandatory retirement dates. While this characteristic is less pronounced for 0-8's, the situation is complicated by the fact that the length of time between promotion to 0-7 and promotion to 0-8 varies extensively. In other words, the assignment patterns of junior 0-8's would be little more enlightening than those of 0-7's. While the same observation does not apply to senior 0-8's, the lack of readily available statistics on seniority among 0-8's makes it infeasible to discriminate intelligently among them. In any case, it seems reasonable to assume that the more senior 0-8's are more or less evenly distributed among the various categories, so that their inclusion or omission should not significantly alter the patterns of assignment as determined for 0-9's and 0-10's during the course of their service as general officers.

(b) As a practical matter, it is obviously desirable to reduce the number of individual assignment patterns considered to the minimum number consistent with valid findings.

5

(3) Analysis of the assignment patterns of the 45 0-9's resulted in an assignment pattern for a composite 0-9. This pattern is displayed in Appendix C, Table II, "Composite 0-9," which shows that the service of the composite 0-9 is divided almost evenly, with 49.8 percent spent in Category I, II, and III assignments and 50.2 percent spent in Category IV and V assignments.

(4) Conclusions regarding the individual service of the 45 0-9's are displayed in Appendix C, Table III, "Individual Patterns of 0-9 Service as General Officers."

(a) There was no single category in which all 0-9's had served, although only two individuals (the Chief of Engineers and the Surgeon General) had served in only one category. Of the remaining 43, 33 had served in at least three categories.

(b) All but three of the 45 0-9's had served both in Category I, II, and III assignments and in Category IV and V assignments. Two of the three exceptions (the Chief of Engineers and the Surgeon General) are specialists, with all their general officer service in Category V (Branch Material) assignments. The third exception spent all of his general officer service in Category IV (Operations/Tactics) or Category V (Branch Material) assignments.

(5) Analysis of the assignment patterns of the 13 0-10's considered resulted in an assignment pattern for a composite 0-10. This pattern is displayed in Appendix C, Table IV, "Composite 0-10." Table IV shows that well over half (59.5 percent) of the composite 0-10's service as a general officer had spent in Category I, II, and III assignments. (The fact that Table IV is based on only 13 individuals should be borne in mind in making comparisons between percentages.)

(6) Conclusions regarding the individual general officer service of the 13 0-10's are displayed in Appendix C, Table V, "Individual Patterns of 0-10 Service as General Officers." Significant points revealed by this analysis are that:

(a) The only type of assignment in which all 13 0-10's had served was Category I (Policy/Strategy). However, all but one of the 0-10's had also served in Category IV (Operations/Tactics) assignments.

(b) All 0-10's had served in at least two categories, and eight had served in three categories. All 0-10's had served both in Category I, II, and III assignments and in Category IV and V assignments.

(7) The assignment patterns of the 0-9's and 0-10's, combined into a composite, or average, are shown in Appendix C, Table VI, "Composite 0-9/0-10." This tabulation shows that slightly more than half (52.7 percent)

of the general officer service of the composite 0-9/0-10 was spent in Category I, II, and III assignments.

(8) Further analysis of the records of 0-9's and 0-10's revealed that, on the average, 0-9's and 0-10's spent approximately the same amount of time in grade as 0-7's and 0-8's. The exact figures are shown in Appendix C, Table VII, "Average Time in Grade of 0-9's and 0-10's as 0-7's and 0-8's."

(9) Considering individual categories of assignment while serving as 0-7's and 0-8's, considerable variation exists between the assignment patterns of the composite 0-9 and the composite 0-10. These differences are shown in Appendix C, Table VIII, "Assignment Patterns of Composite 0-9's and Composite 0-10's as 0-7's and 0-8's."

(a) Two possible explanations for these variations can be suggested: one is that the 0-10's do not include specialists, for which the senior rank normally attained is 0-9; another is that the Army's requirements varied between the time that the present 0-10's were 0-7's and 0-8's and the time that the present 0-9's were in those grades.

(b) It is noteworthy, however, that when the service as 0-7's and 0-8's is combined, and when the categories are grouped, the difference between the patterns for 0-9's and 0-10's becomes considerably less marked. The respective figures are shown in Appendix C, Table IX, "Percentage of Service of Composite 0-9's and Composite 0-10's in Category I, II, and III as 0-7's and 0-8's."

(c) Although the basis of comparison is not exact, it is perhaps useful to note, from Table I, that 43.1 percent of officers currently serving as 0-7's, 53.9 percent of the officers currently serving as 0-8's, and 47.6 percent of the current 0-7's and 0-8's combined are serving in Category I, II, or III assignments.

c. The preceding statistical analysis appears to justify the following conclusions:

(1) In terms both of the assignments being currently filled by general officers and of the assignment patterns of 0-9's and 0-10's during their service as general officers, assignments are about evenly divided between Policy/Strategy, Management/Administration, and MAAG-Mission-Military Diplomacy responsibilities (Categories I, II, and III) on the one hand; and on the other, Operations/Tactics and Branch Material responsibilities (Categories IV and V).

(2) It is worth noting that the higher the rank, the greater the percentage of involvement in Category I, II, and III assignments.

(3) With regard to 0-9's and 0-10's, almost all (56 out of 58 considered) had served as a general officer in more than one category, most typically (29 of the 58 considered) in three categories. All of the

7

13 O-10's and 42 of the 45 O-9's had served both in Category I, II, and III assignments and in Category IV and V assignments.

(4) Thus it appears that the Senior Service College curricula are the chief source of the formal professional educational background both for a substantial portion of all current general officer assignments and a substantial portion of the assignments filled throughout their service as generals by those general officers who were considered as individuals.

d. Ways in which the US Army War College curriculum addresses the requirements for formal education for "professional generalship" as delineated by the types of assignments which US Army general officers fill.

(1) In terms of the categories of assignments adopted for this study, the US Army War College curriculum addresses the problems related to Category I, II, and III assignments as follows:

(a) Category I (Policy/Strategy) is addressed by Course 1 (The United States and the International Environment), Course 2 (International Strategic Appraisals), Course 3 (National Defense Decisionmaking and Management), Course 4 (Strategic Military Studies), Course 5 (Military Forces Alternative Studies), Course 6 (National Security Issues), and the Military Strategy Seminar (MSS). Indirectly, it is also supported by the Human Dimensions of Military Professionalism Seminar (HDMPS).

(b) Category II (Management/Administration) is primarily supported by Course 3 and to a significant degree by Course 5 and Course 6.

(c) Category III (MAAGs, Missions, Military Diplomacy) is supported by Course 1, Course 2, Course 5, Course 6, and the MSS.

(2) The problems associated with Category IV and V assignments are less directly addressed, although Course 3, Course 4, Course 5, the MSS, and the HDMPS do address various aspects of the problems involved in these assignments. In any case, the formal professional educational preparation for Category IV and V assignments is provided primarily by the branch schools and the Command and General Staff College.

PART II

TYPES OF ACTIVITY COMMON TO THE DUTIES OF
GENERAL OFFICERS, REGARDLESS OF ASSIGNMENT

1. In this aspect of the study, a different approach was necessarily taken. Short of the collation of the detailed functions of specific general officer assignments, the only feasible approach appeared to be to query senior field grade officers having experience of close official

association with general officers of varying grades. In view of the broad, all-encompassing nature of the types of activity concerned, it is considered that this approach (while doubtless resulting in some omissions) was sufficiently comprehensive for the purposes of this study. Accordingly, a consensus was obtained from officers who, while comparatively few in number, had extensive and expert background in the subject of general officer assignment requirements.

2. Specific types of activity, within the frame of reference considered by this study, deemed to be common to the duties of general officers regardless of specific assignment are discussed below.

a. Management and administration, in some degree, are aspects of any general officer assignment.

b. Within the frame of reference of his relationships with other military personnel, a general officer's influence is such that his judgments of subordinates are crucial to insure both fairness to individuals and the future best interests of the Army. Hence, he needs thorough understanding of the Army's present and developing requirements, and an ability to judge the attributes of individuals accurately and objectively in terms of those requirements.

c. By virtue of his status, each general officer has an especially significant impact upon the impressions of the Army held by the civilian public at large. This applies to what he says, to his conduct of official and semi-official community relations and of his personal affairs, and to the manner in which he is publicly perceived as performing his official military duties.

d. In a related but somewhat distinct sense, Army general officers are the Army's most influential public spokesmen. This function can be expected to increase in significance in proportion to the rank of the general officer. In consequence, judgment as to what to say (and how to say it) is an important requirement of general officers, and reasonable competence in public speaking is a valuable attribute.

e. At one time or another, many general officers will be called upon to testify before congressional committees and to negotiate with individual congressmen. Ability to deal successfully with the Congress is therefore an important requirement.

f. Similarly, dealing with the public information media is a requirement sooner or later facing most general officers, at the local if not at the national level.

g. Particularly for general officers in the Pentagon, but also for more senior general officers in the field, a requirement exists to work successfully with senior appointed civilian officials, recognizing such officials as sharing the soldier's primary interest in national security

but also as influenced by considerations more ecumenical than those normally influencing the professional military man.

h. All five of the preceding types of actions common to general
officers are significantly influenced by the degree of an officer's
effectiveness (as distinct from "mechanical" skill) in oral communication,
taking this term to include persuasiveness, logic of analysis, plausibility,
and choice of terms meaningful to the specific audience.

i. Either as commanders or as members of senior staffs, general
officers require an informed, although not technical, grasp of legal relationships, authorities, and limitations; this should involve an understanding
of the scopes of civilian and military jurisdictions in both their civil and
criminal applications (addressing both national and international legal
aspects), and include the legal obligations and authority as they pertain
not only to the internal government of the Army but also to the Army's
associations with private contractors, civilian communities, the other military services, and the civilian departments and branches of the Government.

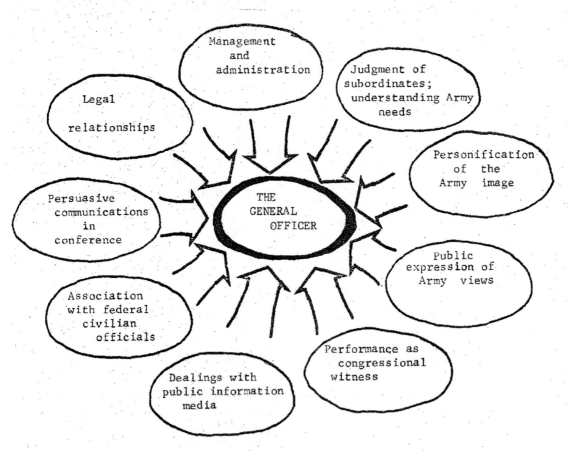

Figure 3. Activities Common to the Duties of General Officer

3. With regard to the types of responsibilities identified as common to general officers, the US Army War College curriculum provides support as follows:

a. Management/Administration is addressed in considerable detail by Course 3, and in general by Course 5 and Course 6.

b. The subject of relationships with military subordinates is a basic element in the HDMPS. Assessment of the developing requirements of the Army is supported by Course 3, Course 4, Course 5, Course 6, and the MSS.

c. The subject of relationships with the civilian public is implicitly supported by the HDMPS, and to a considerable extent by Course 1.

d. Judgment regarding formal public statements is not directly addressed by the US Army War College, nor can it readily be incorporated in any sort of specific terms. Skill in oral presentation does receive some emphasis, at least to the degree that development of such skill is encouraged by the evaluation of oral presentations of committee solutions and SRP's. Training in formal speaking is available to those students enrolled in the Practical Speech Communications Workshop and the Advanced Speech Communications Elective.

e. The subject of dealing with the Congress is addressed only in the general sense that individual congressmen and staff members might be included as guest lecturers in several courses, and that the subjects of group dynamics, interpersonal relationships, and communications are key elements of the HDMPS. No instruction specifically related to the subject of relations between Army officers and the Congress is included in the US Army War College curriculum.

f. Some specific coverage of military relations with the public information media is provided by the Press Panel included in Course 1. While this is useful, it addresses the subject essentially from the viewpoint of the media and consequently does not present the viewpoint of the Army or address the question of techniques and principles involved.

g. The relationship between general officers and senior appointed civilian officials is addressed organizationally in Course 1, and in terms of interpersonal relationships in the HDMPS.

h. Oral communications effectiveness, as described in paragraph 2.h. above, is generally supported by the curriculum as a whole; in certain of its more important aspects, by the HDMPS; and, for some students, by certain electives.

11

i. The subject of legal relationships between general officers in command or senior staff positions within the Army and with other military services, civilian governmental agencies, non-governmental agencies, and civilian communities is not directly addressed by the US Army War College curriculum.

PART III

GENERAL CONCLUSIONS

1. "Professional generalship" can be delineated in terms of the types of assignments filled by US Army generals.

    a. When these types of assignments are grouped according to the portion of the Army educational system which, de facto if not de jure, has primary responsibility for educating officers for them, it can be seen that about half of the assignments depend primarily on the Senior Service College curricula for preparation, the other half depending chiefly upon other aspects of the Army educational system.

    b. The total general officer service of 0-9's and 0-10's shows that about half of this service has been spent in assignments depending for professional educational preparation chiefly upon the Senior Service College curricula. When the records of these officers are studied on an individual basis, it is seen that, with insignificant exceptions, all 0-9's and 0-10's have served both in assignments depending chiefly on background provided by the Senior Service Colleges and in assignments depending chiefly on background provided by the other elements of the Army education system.

2. "Professional generalship" can also be delineated in terms of activities required of general officers regardless of their specific assignments at any given time.

3. An assessment of the US Army War College curriculum in terms of the assignments filled by US Army generals shows that the curriculum addresses, in several ways and with apparent adequacy, all the categories of assignments identified as depending for professional educational background primarily on the Senior Service College curricula.

4. With regard to the responsibilities identified as common to the status of general officer, these do not fall clearly into the province of any specific level of Army education; but the US Army War College, as the senior level of the Army School System and the Army school most directly concerned with qualifying senior officers as a group for the responsibilities of general officers, appears to have major responsibility in this regard. In some cases directly, in others only indirectly, the US Army War College

curriculum addresses most of these responsibilities. In particular, however, the question of relations with the Congress is not addressed at all; relations with the public information media are not addressed adequately; the development of skill in public speaking would benefit by greater, or at least more sharply focused, emphasis; and the question of legal responsibilities of general officers receives no coverage. See Figure 4.

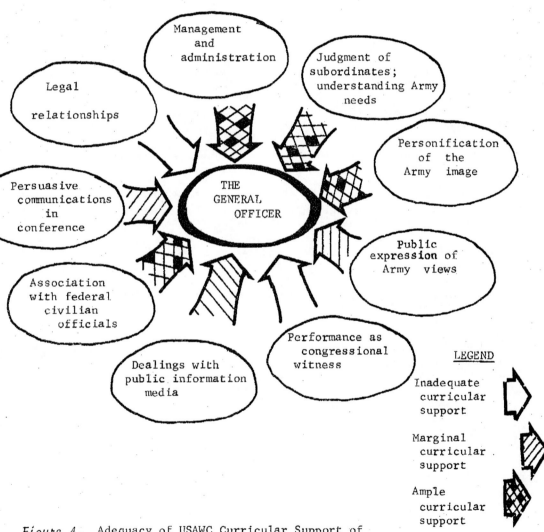

Figure 4. Adequacy of USAWC Curricular Support of "Professional Generalship"

13

PART IV

RECOMMENDATIONS

1. That the US Army War College incorporate into its curriculum (probably most logically during Course 3 or Course 4) a panel composed of the Chief of Legislative Liaison and up to three of his key assistants, to discuss--in one session--procedures, rules, pitfalls, and techniques related to dealings by senior Army officers with the Congress.

2. That the US Army War College incorporate into its curriculum (perhaps during Course 1, but with at least equal logic during Course 3) a panel composed of the Chief of Information and up to three of his key assistants, to discuss--in one session--policies relating to relations with the public information media and, from the point of view of the senior Army officer, the hazards, governing principles, regulations, and inherent opportunities pertaining to such relations.

3. That the attainment of improved oral presentation capability be emphasized through the following procedures:

a. Faculty counselors, from the outset, should stress the importance of this attribute to their student counselees.

b. The Academic Feeder Report should be modified by incorporating a section for specific comment on the effectiveness of the student's oral communication in terms of mechanics, content, and persuasiveness; this section would be in addition to the present form's section dealing with formal presentations. In order to encourage frankness in course advisers' evaluations it should be made clear to all faculty members that (1) faculty counselors will explicitly and promptly counsel their counselees regarding such deficiencies; and (2) the overall evaluation of the student in this regard in the final academic report will be based not on the individual Academic Feeder Reports but on the degree of skill revealed in the final course feeder report.

c. All students would be advised at the initial orientation concerning the importance which the USAWC places on this capability.

4. That the subcourse on "Senior Officers' Law Orientation," taught by a team from The Judge Advocate General's School, which is currently under consideration, be incorporated into the curriculum during Course 5 for Academic Year 1972 (possibly shifted to Course 3 in subsequent academic years) as an integral element in which all US Army War College students participate.

US ARMY WAR COLLEGE
Carlisle Barracks, Pennsylvania

AWCIR   25 June 1971

MEMORANDUM THRU: DI
                 DCOMDT

FOR: COMDT

SUBJECT: Definition of "Professional Generalship."

1. Since the development of qualities of "Professional Generalship" is a key objective of the USAWC curriculum, and since the term "generalship" is fraught with emotional and subjective overtones, I propose that DR&S undertake a study with the dual but related purposes of: (a) defining in comparatively precise terms what "professional generalship" can be considered to encompass; and (b) determining the extent to which the USAWC curriculum addresses the various aspects of "professional generalship" as so defined.

2. My plan for approaching the definition—more properly, perhaps, the delineation—of "professional generalship" has two dimensions:

   a. Determining what, in fact, US Army generals do.

   (1) Using any recent issue of the monthly General Officers' Assignment list, the positions for which general officers are authorized would be categorized in comparatively broad terms such as "Operations/Tactics," "Policy/Strategy," "Management/Administration," "Specialist," etc. Also the number of generals in each category, by grade, would be shown. I recognize that in many gray areas delineation would be arbitrary; and further, that almost any category would involve the application of knowledge and skills pertaining to one or more of the others. (For the proposed approach to dealing with this aspect of the issue, see paragraph 2a(2) below.) Nonetheless, such categorization could be expected to demonstrate the spectrum of areas or fields in which general officers must function.

   (2) Identify, again in broad terms, major functional responsibilities pertaining to more than one of the categories identified.

   (3) Using official biographies of all active duty 3-star and 4-star Army officers, trace each such officer's assignment experience, as a

Appendix A   A-1

general officer, by category. (Limitation of this aspect of the study
to 3-star and 4-star officers would be explained on rational as well as
pragmatic grounds.) This examination could be expected to show that except for specialists, no 3-star or 4-star officer will, except very
abnormally spend his general officer service exclusively or even predom-
inantly in one category. (If this hypothesis proves correct, useful
ammunition should be developed to meet the General Bruce Clarke-General
Ralph Haines arguments.)

    b. Using literature in the field of academic research on leadership,
identify the system of values we should adopt in distinguishing good or
successful leaders from others, and define the behavioral patterns which
characterize those who are "good leaders."

3. Having answered the questions of "What do generals actually do" and
"What system of values distinguishes good leaders," I would compare the
answers with the USAWC curriculum to determine the extent to which the
curriculum contributes to the development of the qualifications and value
system in question.

4. If, as a result, the AY 72 Curriculum appears to be deficient in any
of these fields, consideration could be given to determining what modifi-
cations might be desirable.

5. Request guidance regarding the acceptability of the approach outlined
above.

                                         JOHN B. B. TRUSSELL, JR.
                                         Colonel, ADA
                                         Chairman, Department of
                                         Research and Studies

APPENDIX B

CATEGORIES OF US ARMY GENERAL OFFICER ASSIGNMENTS

1. In categorizing general officer assignments, it is granted that more detailed analysis of the functions of some specific assignments might suggest their being shifted to a category other than the one in which they are listed (e.g., a corps chief of staff is listed under Category IV rather than Category II; although his assignment is of a management/administration nature, the activities which he is managing/administering are preponderantly of an operations/tactics character). Also, the allocation by category is in some respects arbitrary, in that almost any assignment peformed by a general officer entails such a breadth of responsibilities as to involve important aspects of more than one of these categories (e.g., "management/administration" is a feature in practically all general officer assignments). Further, Category V includes assignments which could equally well be listed under one or another of the other categories, depending upon the branch concerned and the nature of the particular assignment (e.g., the Commandant of the Engineer School does not fit completely into any of the other categories; on the other hand, if that assignment is to be segregated into its own category, it seems logical that a corps artillery commander should be similarly segregated, even though he could quite properly be listed under Category IV). However, in all cases the principle employed has been to categorize an assignment in such a way as to contribute ultimately to a meaningful answer to the question: "In what ways does the US Army War College curriculum address the requirements of formal education for 'professional generalship'?"

2. Category I (Policy/Strategy).

   a. General: Assignments dealing primarily with matters of international, national, DOD, joint, and DA policy and/or strategy.

   b. Specific:

   OSD, OJCS: Chief, US Army Element, OSD; WSEG; OASD (MP&R); OASD (ISA); NATO Military Committee; Deputy Director, Defense Supply Agency; DIA; Defense Attaches; OCJCS; Office, Director of the Joint Staff; Office of J-3; Office of J-4; Office of J-5; Joint Continental Defense Integration Planning Staff; CENTO; Peace Delegation, Paris; IADB.

   OSA: OCINFO; CLL; OASA (I&L).

   OCSA: CSA; VCSA; AVCSA; Director of Military Support; Director, Planning and Programs Analysis; Director, Management Information Systems; SAMVA; Safeguard System Manager (and Deputy).

ODCSPER: DCSPER; Asst DCSPER; Director of Plans, Studies &
Budget; Director of Procurement and Distribution; Director
of Individual Training (and Deputy); Director of Military
Personnel Policies; Director of Personnel Systems.

ODCSOPS: DCSOPS; Asst DCSOPS; Director of International &
Civil Affairs (and Deputy); Director of Operations (and
Deputy); Director of Plans (and Deputy).

ODCSLOG: DCSLOG; Special Asst to DCSLOG; Asst DCSLOG;
Asst DCSLOG (Programs & Budget); Asst DCSLOG (Doctrine &
Systems); Asst DCSLOG (Supply & Maintenance); Director of
Installations; Director of Plans.

OCRD: CRD; Deputy CRD; Director of Plans and Programs;
Director of Development; Director of Army Research; Director of Missiles and Space.

OCOA: COA; Asst Comptroller for Finance; Director of Management, Review & Analysis; Director of Army Budget; Asst
Director of Army Budget.

OCORC: CORC; Deputy CORC.

OACSFOR: ACSFOR; Deputy ACSFOR; Director of Air Defense;
Director of CBR & Nuclear Operations; Director, Systems
Directorate; Director, Doctrine & Command Systems Direc-
torate; Director of Organization, Unit Training and
Readiness; Director of Manpower & Forces; Director of Army
Aviation.

OACSI: ACSI; Deputy AC'sSI.

USAWC: Commandant; Deputy Commandant.

CDC: CG; Deputy CG; Chief of Staff; Institute of Land Combat.

SOUTHCOM: CINCSOUTH; J-3.

SHAPE: SACEUR; Chief, Policy Branch; Chief, Nuclear Activities Branch; Exec to SACEUR.

EUCOM: Chief of Staff; J-1; J-3; J-4.

PACOM: Chief of Staff; ACSLOG; ACSPlans.

USARPAC: CINCUSARPAC; Deputy CINCUSARPAC; DCSPER; DCSI;
DCSLOG; DCS Comptroller.

UNC: CINCUNC; Special Asst to CINCUNC.

White House Staff: Special Assistant to the President;
  Special Assistant to the Vice President.

Alaskan Command.

3. Category II (Management/Administration).

    a. General: Assignments concerned with the procurement and alloca-
tion of resources, and direction of the utilization of these resources other
than in a primarily tactical or highly technical sense.

    b. Specific:

Defense Supply Agency Field Activities.

OSA: Director, Army Council of Review Boards.

OCSA: Safeguard System Command; US Army Computer Systems
  Command; SGS.

ODCSPER: USA Physical Disability Agency; USA Recruiting Command.

Chief, Army Audit Agency.

The Inspector General.

OPO.

CONARC: CG; Deputy CG; Staff.

CONUS Armies: CG's; Deputy CG's; Staffs.

USAG, Fort Hamilton, N.Y.

Fort Devens, Mass.

US Army Aviation Schools.

Fort Benjamin Harrison.

MDW.

AMC: CG; Deputy CG; Staff; CG, Natick Labs; CG, Deseret Test
  Center; CG, Mobility Equipment Command; Army Aviation
  Systems Command; Army Missile Command; Test and Evaluation
  Command; White Sands Missile Range.

US Forces, Japan.

US Army Japan.

NSA.

OCMH.

ASA.

4. Category III (MAACs, Missions, Military Diplomacy).

a. General: Assignments, other than those involving formulation of overall policy or strategy, in which international military cooperation is the dominant consideration.

b. Specific:

Defense Representative, India.

US Military Delegation, Brazil.

Governor of the Canal Zone.

AFSOUTH.

Allied Land Forces, Southern Europe.

LANDSOUTHEAST.

AFCENT.

EUCOM: Military Assistance Directorate.

MAACs and Missions.

US Commander, Berlin.

MACV: Deputy Commander; Chief of Staff; Joint Staff; ACS for Military Assistance; Military Regions; CORDS; Special Assistant to COMUSMACV; DCS for Economic Affairs; Military Equipment Delivery Team, Cambodia.

Military Assistance Command, Thailand.

US Army Support, Thailand.

US Army, Ryukyu Islands.

5. Category IV (Operations/Tactics).

a. General: Assignments in which the predominant activity involves tactical military operations in the field or training therefor (less branch material assignments).

b. Specific:

Defense Communications Planning Group.

USMA: Superintendent; Commandant of Cadets.

CGSC: Commandant; Assistant Commandant.

Training Centers.

DDR&E: Tac Warfare Program Directorate.

Corps: Commanders; Chiefs of Staff; Corps Support Commands.

Division: Commanders; Assistant Division Commanders.

Commandant, John F. Kennedy Center.

Project MASSTER.

CDC: Combat Support Group; Combat Service Support Group;
    CDEC; Combat Arms Group.

US Army, Alaska.

US Army Forces Southern Command.

CENTAG: Chief of Staff.

USAREUR: CINC; Chief of Staff; DCSPER; DCSI; DCSOPS; DCSLOG;
    Comptroller; CG Seventh US Army Troops; TASCOMs; USAMC, Europe.

USMACV: CG; Delta Regional Assistance Command.

USARV: Deputy CG; General Staff; Regional Assistance Commands;
    Aviation Brigades; Support Commands.

US Army Hawaii: CG.

Log Commands.

Eighth US Army: Deputy CG; General Staff; Korea Support Command.

STRICOM.

6. Category V (Branch Material).

    a. General: Assignments reserved to general officers of a specific
arm or service.

B-5

b. Specific:

OASD (Health and Environment): Deputy ASD.

OASD (Installations and Logistics): Assistant for Construction Operations; Director for Ground and Air Ammunition; Director for Ships and Equipment.

Defense Communications Agency.

JCS: Deputy Director, J-6.

ODCSLOG: Director of Ammunition.

OACS, C-E.

TAG.

CG, US Army Administration Center.

OCCH.

CG, US Army Finance Center.

OTJAG.

OPMG.

Medical Corps, Dental Corps, Army Nurse Corps, Medical Specialist. Corps, Veterinary Corps.

OCE.

Division Engineers.

Construction Directorate, MACV.

USMA: Dean of the Academic Board.

Branch Schools: Commandants; Assistant Commandants.

STRATCOM.

Military Traffic Management and Terminal Service.

AMC: Weapons Command; Munitions Command; Tank-Automotive Command; Electronics Command.

NORAD.

ARADCOM.

USAREUR: Engineer; Provost Marshal; Judge Advocate; AG;
USA Engineer Command; Electronics Command.

ADA Commands and brigades.

FA brigades.

Corps artillery commanders.

Separate infantry brigades.

MACV: Surgeon.

USARV: Engineer Construction Agency; MP Brigade.

Eighth US Army: Engineer.

Director, WAC.

Army and Air Force Exchange System.

TABLES

TABLE I - DISTRIBUTION OF GENERAL OFFICERS BY GRADE

Category	0-10	0-9	0-8	0-7	Total	% of Total GO's
I (Policy/Strategy)	7	22	45	46	120	23.3
II (Management/Administration)	2	7	40	47	96	18.6
III (MAAGs, Missions, Military Diplomacy)	2	2	18	22	44	8.5
IV (Operations/Tactics)	2	11	42	68	123	23.8
V (Branch Material)	-	3	46	84	133	25.8
TOTALS	13	45	191	267	516	100.0

TABLE II - COMPOSITE 0-9

Category	Average Months	% of Total Time
I (Policy/Strategy)	31.8	29.5
II (Management/Administration)	13.4	12.5
III (MAAGs, Missions, Military Diplomacy)	8.4	7.8
IV (Operations/Tactics)	38.7	35.9
V (Branch Material)	15.3	14.2
TOTAL	107.6	99.9

TABLE III - INDIVIDUAL PATTERNS OF O-9 SERVICE AS GENERAL OFFICERS

Category	Number of O-9's Who Have Served in Category	% of O-9's
I (Policy/Strategy)	34	80.0
II (Management/Administration)	23	51.1
III (MAAGs, Missions, Military Diplomacy)	15	33.3
IV (Operations/Tactics)	39	86.7
V (Branch Material)	22	48.9

Number of Different Categories in Which Served	Number of O-9's
5	2
4	10
3	21
2	10
1	2
TOTAL	45

TABLE IV - COMPOSITE O-10

Category	Average Months	% of Total Time
I (Policy/Strategy)	70.5	45.3
II (Management/Administration)	10.9	7.0
III (MAAGs, Missions, Military Diplomacy)	11.2	7.2
IV (Operations/Tactics)	60.9	39.1
V (Branch Material)	2.2	1.4
TOTALS	155.7	100.0

TABLE V - INDIVIDUAL PATTERNS OF O-10's SERVICE AS GENERAL OFFICERS

Category	Number of O-10's Who Have Served in Category	% of O-10's
I (Policy/Strategy)	13	100.0
II (Management/Administration)	6	46.1
III MAAGs, Missions, Military Diplomacy	8	61.5
IV (Operations/Tactics)	12	92.3
V (Branch Material)	3	23.1

Number of Different Categories in Which Served	Number of O-10's
5	0
4	4
3	8
2	1
1	0
TOTAL	13

TABLE VI - COMPOSITE O-9/O-10

Category	Average Months	% of Total Time
I (Policy/Strategy)	40.5	34.3
II (Management/Administration)	12.8	10.8
III (MAAGs, Missions, Military Diplomacy)	9.0	7.6
IV (Operations/Tactics)	43.5	36.8
V (Branch Material)	12.4	10.5
TOTALS	118.2	100.0

TABLE VII - AVERAGE TIME IN GRADE OF O-9's AND O-10's AS O-7's AND O-8's

	Average Time in Grade (Months) as		
	O-7	O-8	O-7 + O-8
Composite O-9	35.2	46.9	82.1
Composite O-10	38.6	46.4	85.0

TABLE VIII - ASSIGNMENT PATTERNS OF COMPOSITE 0-9's AND COMPOSITE 0-10's

AS 0-7's AND 0-8's.

		Percent of Service		
Category		As 0-7	As 0-8	As 0-7 + 0-8
I (Policy/Strategy)	0-9's	20.5	26.9	24.1
	0-10's	52.6	39.2	45.3
II (Management/Administration)	0-9's	12.8	12.2	12.4
	0-10's	4.9	4.1	4.5
III (MAAGs, Missions,	0-9's	10.2	7.9	8.9
Military Diplomacy)	0-10's	0.0	8.6	4.7
IV (Operations/Tactics)	0-9's	34.4	40.7	38.0
	0-10's	36.8	48.1	42.9
V (Branch Material)	0-9's	22.2	12.4	16.6
	0-10's	5.7	0.0	2.6

TABLE IX - PERCENTAGE OF SERVICE OF COMPOSITE 0-9's AND COMPOSITE 0-10's

AS 0-7's AND 0-8's.

	Percentage of Service Spent in Categories I, II, and III as		
	0-7	0-8	0-7 + 0-8
0-9	43.4	46.9	45.4
0-10	57.5	51.9	54.5

CPSIA information can be obtained at www.ICGtesting.com
Printed in the USA
BVOW07s1934120214

344750BV00010B/318/P